MATH ADVENTURES

Ocean Giants

by Wendy Clemson
and David Clemson

Math and curriculum
consultant: Debra Voege, M.A.,
science and math curriculum
resource teacher

GARETH**STEVENS**
GS
PUBLISHING
A Member of the WRC Media Family of Companies

Please visit our web site at: www.garethstevens.com
For a free color catalog describing Gareth Stevens Publishing's list of high-quality books
and multimedia programs, call 1-800-542-2595 (USA) or 1-800-387-3178 (Canada).
Gareth Stevens Publishing's fax: (414) 332-3567

Library of Congress Cataloging-in-Publication Data available upon request from publisher.
Fax (414) 336-0157 for the attention of the Publishing Records Department.

ISBN-13: 978-0-8368-7840-0 (lib. bdg.)
ISBN-13: 978-0-8368-8139-4 (softcover)

This North American edition first published in 2007 by
Gareth Stevens Publishing
A Member of the WRC Media Family of Companies
330 West Olive Street, Suite 100
Milwaukee, WI 53212 USA

This U.S. edition copyright © 2007 by Gareth Stevens, Inc. Original edition copyright © 2007 by ticktock
Entertainment Ltd. First published in Great Britain in 2006 by ticktock Media Ltd., Unit 2, Orchard Business Centre,
North Farm Road, Tunbridge Wells, Kent, TN2 3XF

ticktock project editor: Rebecca Clunes
ticktock project designer: Sara Greasley
Gareth Stevens editor: Tea Benduhn
Gareth Stevens art direction: Tammy West
Gareth Stevens graphic designer: Kami Strunsee
Gareth Stevens production: Jessica Yanke and Robert Kraus

Picture credits
t=top, b=bottom, c=center, l=left, r=right
age fotostock/Super Stock 11, 17t, 24-25, 30; Alan Briere/SuperStock 13b; David B. Fleetham/SeaPics.com
15, 19; Bob Gibbons/Science Photo Library 21; Richard Hermann/SeaPics.com 18; IFAW International Fund for
Animal Welfare/J. Gordon 22l; Mike Johnson/earthwindow.com 23; Lon E. Lauber, Alaska Image Library, United States
Fish and Wildlife Service 10; Kevin Raskoff, California State University, Monterey Bay/NOAA 14t; Shutterstock
1, 2, 4tl, 4bl, 4br, 5, 6, 8-9, 14b, 20b, 26, 27, 31t, 31b, 32; Ticktock Media archives 13t, 17b, 22r; U.S. Army 4tr;
James D. Watt/SeaPics.com 28-29.

Printed in Canada

1 2 3 4 5 6 7 8 9 10 10 09 08 07 06

CONTENTS

Under the Ocean 4

Going Diving 6

Supertankers and Big Ships 8

North Pole Animals 10

Orcas on the Move 12

Avoiding the Jellyfish 14

Shark Attack! 16

Giant Octopus and Squid 18

The Wandering Albatross 20

Whale Watching 22

Playful Dolphins 24

The Manta Ray 26

Your Last Dive 28

Tips and Help 30

Answers 32

MEASUREMENT CONVERSIONS

1 inch = 2.5 centimeters	1 ton = 0.9 tonne
1 foot = 0.3 meters	1 pint = 0.5 liter
1 mile = 1.6 kilometers	1 quart = 1 liter
1 ounce = 28.3 grams	1 gallon = 3.8 liters
1 pound = .05 kilogram	

UNDER THE OCEAN

You have an exciting job. You are a deep-sea diver! You explore amazing underwater worlds full of giant creatures. You see enormous fish, octopuses, and whales during your dives. You travel all over the world, diving in warm and cold waters. It is time to start a new trip!

Being a deep-sea diver is an exciting and important job.

A diver sometimes has to look for a sunken ship and find out what made it sink.

Sometimes, things, such as pipes, need to be fixed underwater.

Divers can be scientists who study fish, plants, rocks, and ocean water.

Divers take pictures underwater. The pictures are used in films, television programs, and advertisements.

Did you know that deep-sea divers need to use math?

Inside this book, you will find math puzzles that divers have to solve every day. You will also have a chance to answer number questions about ocean animals.

What is inside the book?

Find out what needs to be done in your busy day.

Charts and tables will help you answer the math questions.

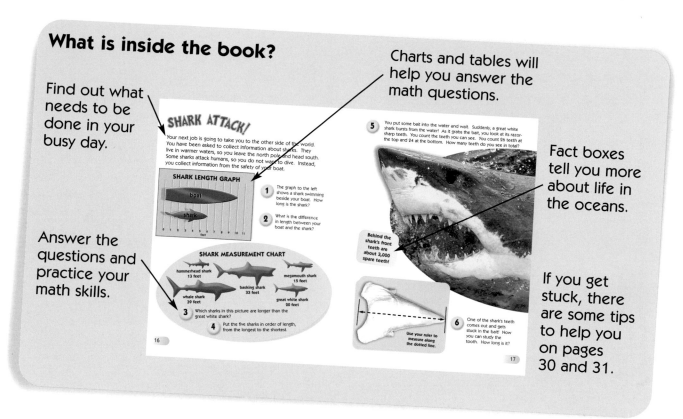

Fact boxes tell you more about life in the oceans.

Answer the questions and practice your math skills.

If you get stuck, there are some tips to help you on pages 30 and 31.

Are you ready to be a deep-sea diver?

You will need paper, a pencil, and a ruler, and don't forget to bring your diving suit. Let's go!

GOING DIVING

The ocean is cold. You need to wear a thick diving suit to stay warm. You also wear a mask and flippers. An air tank on your back lets you breathe underwater. Lead weights stop you from floating upward!

The box to the right shows some of your diving equipment.

1 Is the air hose above or below the air tanks?

2 What is to the right of the flippers?

3 What is directly above the face mask?

DIVING EQUIPMENT

air hose   flippers   lead weight

face mask   air tanks

Most dives last about one hour, but some jobs take longer. You could be underwater for two, three, or even four hours.

You see lots of creatures underwater. You can keep a record of what you see underwater, using a map like the one below.

UNDERWATER MAP

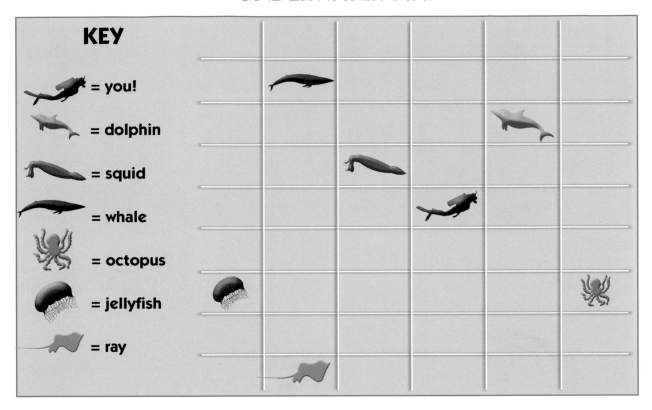

KEY

= you!

= dolphin

= squid

= whale

= octopus

= jellyfish

= ray

Use the Underwater Map above to answer the questions below. To reach the dolphin, you have to move 2 squares up and 1 square to the right. Another way to get there is to move 1 square to the right and 2 squares up.

4 How would you move to reach the whale?

5 How would you move to get to the jellyfish?

6 The ray is 4 squares down and 2 squares to your right — true or false?

SUPERTANKERS AND BIG SHIPS

You are on a ship that will take you to your diving spot. You look out over the ocean and see a supertanker. It is a ship that carries barrels of oil around the world. Supertankers are huge! They are ocean giants made by humans.

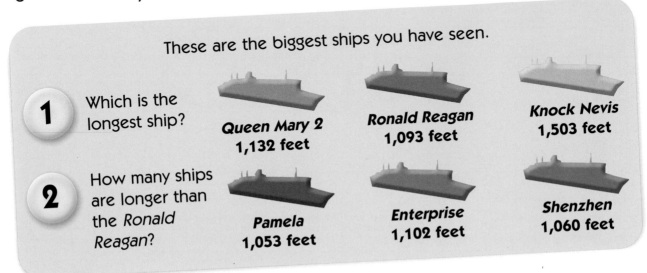

These are the biggest ships you have seen.

1 Which is the longest ship?

Queen Mary 2
1,132 feet

Ronald Reagan
1,093 feet

Knock Nevis
1,503 feet

2 How many ships are longer than the *Ronald Reagan*?

Pamela
1,053 feet

Enterprise
1,102 feet

Shenzhen
1,060 feet

The speed of a ship is measured in knots. One knot is about 1 mile per hour, so a ship traveling at 30 knots is going about 30 miles per hour.

SHIP SPEED CHART

name of ship	speed in knots
Queen Mary 2	30
Pamela	26
Ronald Reagan	30
Enterprise	$33\frac{1}{2}$
Knock Nevis	16
Shenzhen	25

3 Which is the fastest ship?

4 Which ships go at the same speed?

5 Look at the chart to the left and the ships on page 8. Is the longest ship also the slowest?

Supertankers are the biggest ships in the world. They can be $\frac{1}{4}$ mile long.

NORDSTRAUM

NORTH POLE ANIMALS

Your ship heads to the sea near the North Pole. You have been asked to study sea lions and walruses there. You need to find out how deep they dive and what they eat. You find out that these animals are even better at diving than you are!

Sea lions gather near the shore, so they do not have far to go to get into the water.

1 Sea lions can stay underwater for 40 minutes. One sea lion has been underwater for 18 minutes. How much longer can it stay underwater?

2 Sea lions can dive 600 feet below the surface of the water. During your dive, you spot a sea lion 150 feet below the surface of the water. How much farther down can it go?

Male sea lions are about 10 feet long and weigh about one ton.

WHAT DID A WALRUS EAT?

You spend a few days watching a walrus. The bar graph to the right shows what creatures the walrus eats.

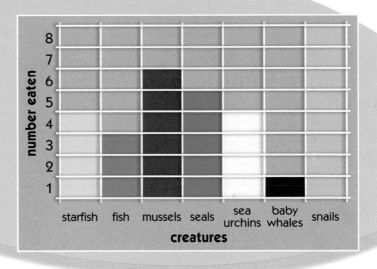

3 How many creatures did the walrus eat in total?

4 How many snails did the walrus eat?

5 Which creatures did the walrus eat four of?

6 What is the difference between the numbers of fish and seals?

ORCAS ON THE MOVE

Your next job is to follow a group of orcas. An orca is the biggest dolphin in the world. It is a fierce hunter that twists and turns in the water to catch fish. You are safe diving with the group of orcas because they do not eat humans.

Orcas swim quickly. They can swim about ½ mile in 1 minute.

1 An orca heads toward a large group of fish. How quickly will it get to them if the fish are 3 miles away?

2 Another orca takes 2 minutes to get to the fish. How far from the fish was it?

The orcas play around your boat, leaping out of the water. When they leap, you can see their black and white patterns. Each orca has a slightly different pattern. Scientists can recognize each orca by its pattern.

3 Scientists need to be good at identifying patterns. Look at the patterns below. In each of them, which color square comes next — black or white?

A

B

C

D

4 Orcas live in small groups. The first group you see has 5 orcas in it. As you watch, 2 of them leave. Then, a second group of 9 orcas joins the first. How many orcas are there now?

Female orcas are about 23 feet long. Male orcas are bigger. They are about 26 feet long.

AVOIDING THE JELLYFISH

It is time to get back into the icy water. You are diving to find one of the world's largest jellyfish. It is called the lion's mane jellyfish. You do not have to dive down far before you see the jellyfish. It is very big, almost the same size as you are. You stay far away from its tentacles — if they touch your skin, they will sting!

1 There are many different types of jellyfish in the ocean. You draw pictures of the types you see. You draw lines connecting the jellyfish that are the same type. What shapes did you draw?

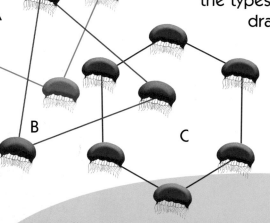

A

B

C

The lion's mane jellyfish has long, floating tentacles. Just one tentacle can be more than 115 feet long!

2 What are the whole numbers that come between 110 and 115?

3 How many fives are in 115?

4 A lion's mane jellyfish lives for about one year. How many days is that?

5 You see a lion's mane jellyfish that is about 2 months old. Approximately how many days old is it?

A jellyfish does not have a brain, a heart, eyes, ears, or bones.

SHARK ATTACK!

Your next job is going to take you to the other side of the world. You have been asked to collect information about sharks. They live in warmer waters, so you leave the north pole and head south. Some sharks attack humans, so you do not want to dive. Instead, you collect information from the safety of your boat.

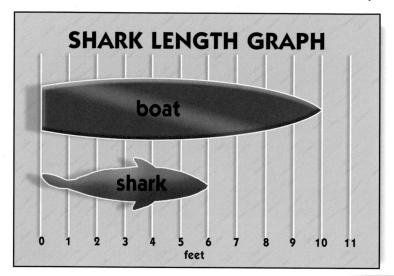

SHARK LENGTH GRAPH

boat

shark

0 1 2 3 4 5 6 7 8 9 10 11
feet

1 The graph to the left shows a shark swimming beside your boat. How long is the shark?

2 What is the difference in length between your boat and the shark?

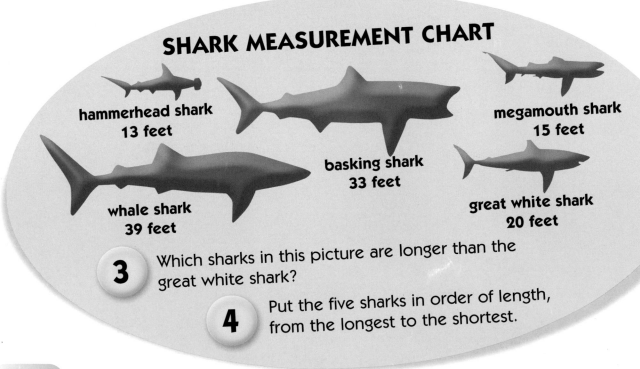

SHARK MEASUREMENT CHART

hammerhead shark
13 feet

megamouth shark
15 feet

basking shark
33 feet

whale shark
39 feet

great white shark
20 feet

3 Which sharks in this picture are longer than the great white shark?

4 Put the five sharks in order of length, from the longest to the shortest.

5 You put some bait into the water and wait. Suddenly, a great white shark bursts out of the water! As it grabs the bait, you look at its razor-sharp teeth. You count the teeth you can see. You count 26 teeth at the top and 24 at the bottom. How many teeth do you see in total?

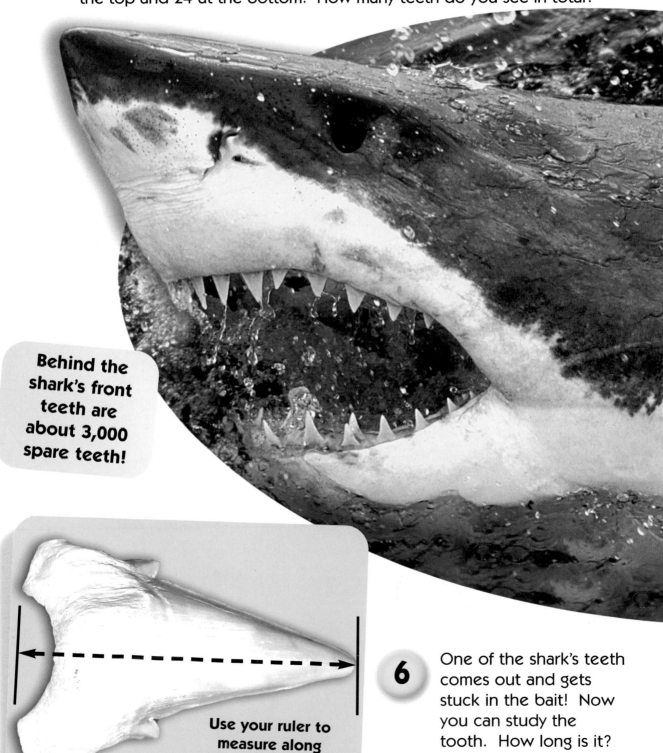

Behind the shark's front teeth are about 3,000 spare teeth!

Use your ruler to measure along the dotted line.

6 One of the shark's teeth comes out and gets stuck in the bait! Now you can study the tooth. How long is it?

GIANT OCTOPUS AND SQUID

You now head away from the coast, into deeper waters. You are looking for two of the most mysterious creatures of the ocean: the giant octopus and the giant squid. Very few people have seen the giant octopus, and no one has seen the giant squid alive. You might be lucky enough to see both!

The giant squid really is a giant. It can grow up to 40 feet long! Although no scientists have seen one alive, they can guess the giant squid's length from its remains found in whales' stomachs. Scientists know the giant squid looks similar to the squid shown on the right.

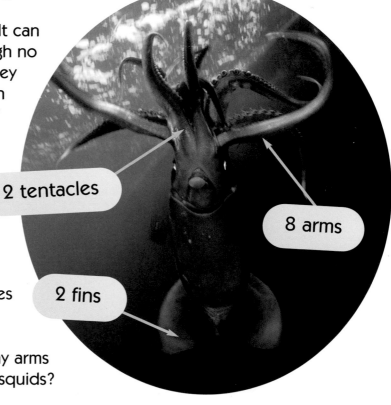

2 tentacles

8 arms

2 fins

1 How many fins are on 4 squids?

2 How many tentacles are on 7 squids?

3 How many arms are on 2 squids?

LONGER THAN A BUS

4 One squid is the length of 2 short buses. Look at the row of buses below. How many squids would this measure?

  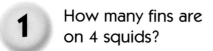 

Giant octopuses can grow up to 30 feet long.

Not only is the giant octopus long, it also weighs a lot. Some octopuses can weigh up to 300 pounds!

OCTOPUS PUZZLES

5 An octopus has 8 arms. Two of the multiplication puzzles below have 8 as the answer. Which puzzles are they?

A
2 x 6 =

B
4 x 4 =

C
8 x 1 =

D
4 x 2 =

E
8 x 10 =

F
3 x 3 =

6 You can also make 8 by adding two numbers. What are the ways you can add two numbers to make 8?

THE WANDERING ALBATROSS

For the last few weeks, you have been far from land, out at sea. Suddenly, you spot a wandering albatross. It is the biggest seabird in the world. You are hundreds of miles from the nearest shore, but that is not a problem for the albatross. It spends years at sea without stopping on land.

A bird's wingspan is measured from the tip of one wing to the tip of the other wing. A wandering albatross can have a wingspan as wide as 11 feet. The albatross you see is a little smaller. It has a wingspan of 8 feet.

WINGSPAN DIAGRAM

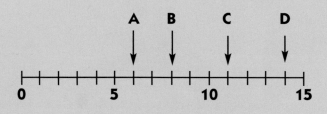

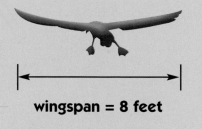

wingspan = 8 feet

1 Look at the number line to the left. Is 8 at A, B, C, or D?

2 Is 11 at A, B, C, or D on the number line?

A wandering albatross is a big bird, and it lays big eggs, too. Its egg is about 4 inches tall. That is as tall as a soup can!

3 How many wandering albatross eggs are needed to equal 1 foot?

Scientists sometimes put tags on birds to track them and to learn more about them. You see five tagged birds. The tags tell you the age of each bird. Their ages are below.

A = 22 years

B = 38 years

C = 14 years

D = 7 years

E = 23 years

4 Round each bird's age, up or down, to the nearest 10.

A wandering albatross can live as long as 80 years.

WHALE WATCHING

Even though whales are giant creatures, they can be hard to find! You are in the Pacific Ocean, in an area where many different kinds of whales have been seen. The next part of your job is to collect information about minke whales and pilot whales.

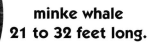

minke whale
21 to 32 feet long.

pilot whale
16 to 20 feet long.

WHICH WHALE?

1 You see lots of whales. Which of the whales below are minke whales and which are pilot whales?

whale A
10 + 14 feet

whale B
1 + 3 + 5 + 7 feet

whale C
40 − 20 feet

whale D
14 + 13 feet

2 Pilot whales live together in groups of up to 50. If there is a group of 50 whales, how many groups of 5 are there?

3 How many pairs of whales are there in a group of 50?

4 The biggest animal on Earth is the blue whale. Below are some amazing facts and measurements about the blue whale. Can you match the correct measurement to each fact?

A It is longer than a tennis court.

B The amount of food it eats every day is equal to the weight of 3 small cars.

C The milk a baby blue whale drinks every day is the same amount as a full bathtub.

25 gallons

9,000 pounds

100 feet

SWIMMING PAST THE GIANT

adult length: 100 feet

5 You see a blue whale, but it does not seem to notice you. You swim past it very slowly. If you travel 10 feet every 10 seconds, how long does it take you to swim the length of the whale?

PLAYFUL DOLPHINS

It is time to head back to shore. As you look out at the ocean, you see an animal leap out of the water. It is a dolphin! Then, you see another! They are having fun, jumping and chasing each other. Two of them are even playing catch with some seaweed!

1 At first, you see 5 dolphins. Then 7 more dolphins join the fun. How many dolphins are there in total?

2 Dolphins live in family groups called pods. There are normally 12 dolphins in a pod. How many groups of 4 dolphins make a pod?

DOLPHIN FACTS

3 Look at the dolphin number facts to the right. Each fact number is the answer to one of the calculations to the right. Match the number facts to the calculation answers.

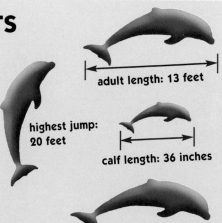

adult length: 13 feet

highest jump: 20 feet

calf length: 36 inches

top speed: 22 miles per hour

A. 15 + 7

B. 78 − 58

C. 19 + 17

D. 21 − 8

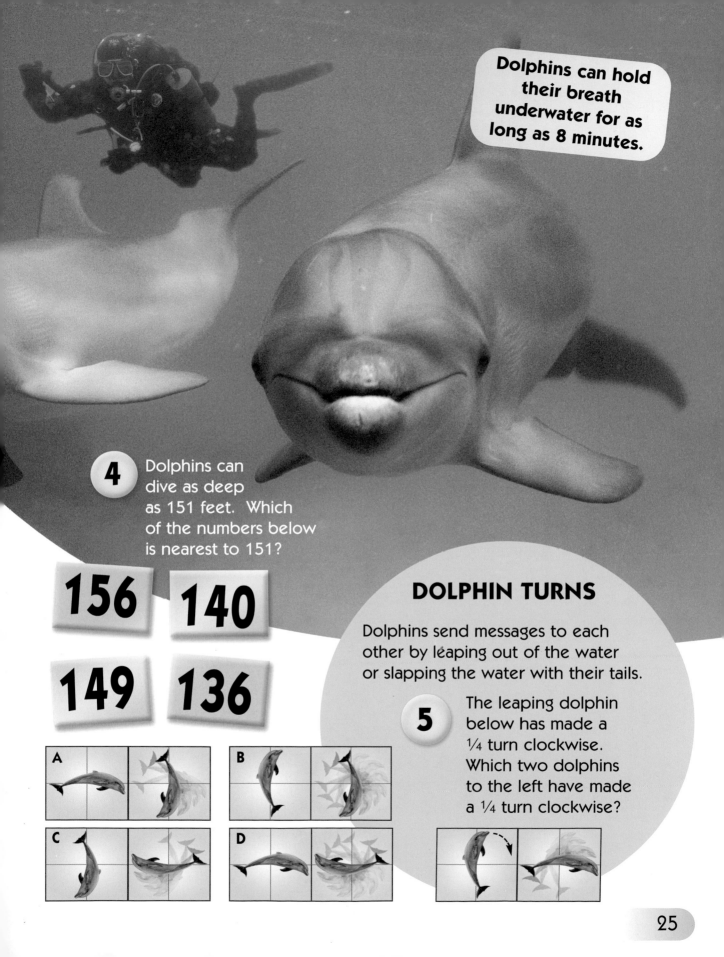

Dolphins can hold their breath underwater for as long as 8 minutes.

4 Dolphins can dive as deep as 151 feet. Which of the numbers below is nearest to 151?

156 **140**

149 **136**

DOLPHIN TURNS

Dolphins send messages to each other by leaping out of the water or slapping the water with their tails.

5 The leaping dolphin below has made a ¼ turn clockwise. Which two dolphins to the left have made a ¼ turn clockwise?

A

B

C

D

THE MANTA RAY

Your boat stops near a coral reef. The reef is a sea garden made from the skeletons of tiny sea animals. The water here is warm, and brightly colored fish swim near you. Suddenly, a giant shadow passes over you. It is a manta ray. It must be at least 22 feet wide!

You have been asked to find out the sizes of the manta rays swimming around you. You catch some rays in a net to weigh and measure them. The table to the right shows your results.

	width	weight
ray 1	14 feet	1,700 pounds
ray 2	18 feet	2,300 pounds
ray 3	20 feet	3,000 pounds

1 Which ray weighs the most?

2 What is the difference in width between ray 1 and ray 3?

3 What is the difference in weight between ray 1 and ray 2?

4 If the purple manta ray to the right turns in a half circle, which of the green manta rays below shows how it will look?

— eye

— fin

— tail

A

B

C

Manta rays swim near the surface of the water. They feed on tiny sea creatures. They are not usually a danger to humans.

YOUR LAST DIVE

You have carried out diving jobs all around the world. This dive to the coral reef is your last dive for this trip. The coral reef is home to many animals. You see lots of tiny, brightly colored fish swimming around. As you watch, a big group of fish swims by. The group, called a school, twists and turns together. It almost looks like one big fish!

FISH DIAGRAM

You see a school of blue and green fish. The diagram below shows how many of each color you see in the school.

1 How many fish are blue?

2 How many fish are green?

3 How many fish are blue and green?

FISH CHART

4 You made a chart of the number of schools of fish you saw on each dive. On which dive did you see the most schools?

5 How many schools did you see in total?

6 How many schools of fish did you see on dive 2?

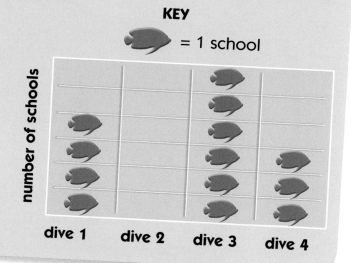

KEY

= 1 school

number of schools

dive 1 dive 2 dive 3 dive 4

It is time to head back to shore. Diving was fun! You will be back in the water soon.

TIPS AND HELP

PAGES 6-7

Grid maps - You find the path for objects on a grid map by moving right or left, then up or down (or up or down and then right or left).

PAGES 8-9

Comparing and ordering - To put numbers such as ships' lengths in order, look at the thousands (one thousand for all these ships), then the hundreds, the tens, and, finally, the units (or ones).

PAGES 10-11

Subtracting (taking away) - Look for ways to make this easier to do. For example, 40 minus 18 can be done as 40 minus 20, which leaves 20, then add 2, to get the answer 22.

Bar graph - Each colored box in the graph means one creature that was eaten. A bar graph helps compare two sets of information. This graph compares how many creatures were eaten and what type of creatures they were.

Find the difference - This is the same as "take away," "minus," or "subtract."

PAGES 12-13

Predicting patterns - When we figure out how a pattern would continue, we are predicting, or imagining, what will happen next. Count the squares and look for a pattern. Then, pretend the same pattern continues across the page. Which color do you think will come next?

PAGES 14-15

Flat shapes - Counting the sides is necessary in naming flat shapes. A triangle has three sides, a rectangle has four sides (with opposite sides that match in length and four right angles), and a hexagon has six sides.

Numbers between - Picture a number line or draw one on a piece of paper. Then you can see the numbers that are missing.

Fives in 115 - Write down all of the "fives" it takes to get to 115: 5, 10, 15, 20, and so on. Then count up how many numbers you have written.

PAGES 16-17

Ordering length - First check that all the items (here the items are sharks) are measured using the same unit of measurement (here they are all measured in feet). Look for the highest tens (whale shark and basking shark). Then check the units (or ones). The whale shark has the highest number, so it is the longest shark. Now find the next lowest number and continue.

Using a ruler - Make sure the "0" on the ruler is exactly at one end of the line that you are measuring, then read what the ruler says at the other end of the line.

PAGES 18-19

Multiplication - Multiplication is the same as "times." We use the "x" sign to mean times. 4 x 2 is the same as 4 times 2 (or 4 two times).

PAGES 20-21

Rounding numbers - When we round a number to the nearest ten, we make numbers ending in 5, 6, 7, 8, or 9 bigger, and we make numbers ending in 1, 2, 3, or 4 smaller. So, 22 is rounded down to 20, but 38 is rounded up to 40.

PAGES 22-23

Math signs - Remember what the math signs mean:
+ means add, plus, or sum
– means take away, minus, or subtract

Measures - Remember, we use quarts, pints, and gallons to measure liquids; pounds and ounces to measure weight; and inches, feet, and miles to measure length.

Timing - If you swim 10 feet in 10 seconds, you swim 10 x 10 feet in 10 x 10 seconds.

PAGES 24-25

Nearest numbers - Count forward and backward from 151. Which number do you reach first? That is the number nearest to 151.

Clockwise - The diagram below shows the direction the hands move on a clock.

PAGES 26-27

Width - When we measure the size of something, we can look at its length (or height) and width. If it is not flat, we can also measure its depth.

Turning around - A full circle is one complete turn. A half circle is half as far around.

PAGES 28-29

Sorting - The diagram is called a Venn diagram. It shows a set of blue fish and a set of green fish. The sets overlap so that the fish with both blue and green on them are in the blue set and in the green set.

Pictogram - In the fish chart, a picture is used as a symbol for information. In this pictogram, a fish shape means one school of fish.

ANSWERS

PAGES 6-7

1 above
2 lead weight
3 air hose
4 three squares up and two squares left or two squares left and three squares up
5 two squares down and three squares left or three squares left and two squares down
6 false – the ray is four squares down and two squares left

PAGES 8-9

1 *Knock Nevis*
2 3 ships
3 *Enterprise*
4 *Queen Mary 2* and *Ronald Reagan*
5 yes

PAGES 10-11

1 22 minutes
2 450 feet
3 31 creatures
4 8 snails
5 starfish and sea urchins
6 2

PAGES 12-13

1 6 minutes
2 1 mile
3 A = white, B = white,
C = black, D = white
4 12 orcas

PAGES 14-15

1 A = square
B = triangle
C = hexagon
2 111, 112, 113, and 114
3 23 fives
4 365 days
5 about 60 days

PAGES 16-17

1 6 feet long
2 4 feet
3 whale shark and basking shark
4 whale shark
basking shark
great white shark
megamouth shark
hammerhead shark
5 50 teeth
6 3½ inches

PAGES 18-19

1 8 fins
2 14 tentacles
3 16 arms
4 2½ squids
5 C (8 x 1) and D (4 x 2)
6 0+8, 1+7, 2+6, 3+5, 4+4, 5+3, 6+2, 7+1, 8+0

PAGES 20-21

1 B
2 C
3 3 eggs
4 A = 20, B = 40, C = 10, D = 10, E = 20

PAGES 22-23

1 A = 24 feet, minke
B = 16 feet, pilot
C = 20 feet, pilot
D = 27 feet, minke
2 10 groups of 5
3 25 pairs
4 A = 100 feet
B = 9,000 pounds
C = 25 gallons
5 100 seconds or 1 minute and 40 seconds

PAGES 24-25

1 12 dolphins
2 3 groups
3 A = top speed
B = highest jump
C = calf length
D = adult length
4 149
5 A and C

PAGES 26-27

1 ray 3
2 6 feet
3 600 pounds
4 B

PAGES 28-29

1 9 blue fish
2 17 green fish
3 6 blue and green fish
4 dive 3
5 13 schools
6 0 (or none)